NOW YOU CAN READ...
DAVID and JONATHAN

STORY RETOLD BY ROSALIND SUTTON

ILLUSTRATED BY RUSSELL LEE

THOMAS NELSON PUBLISHERS · NASHVILLE · CAMDEN · NEW YORK

David was a young shepherd boy. His father had eight sons and he was the youngest. The older boys became soldiers in the king's army. David was left at home to look after the sheep.

One day, a stranger named Samuel came to David's home. He told David that God had chosen David to be a king when he was older. David was surprised, but he did not say anything.

Some time later, David was taken to see the king of the country who was King Saul. David was very good at playing the harp. King Saul liked to listen to him play. He asked David to stay at the palace with him.

David was a gentle boy and a brave one too. Once, a great giant named Goliath, came with his army against King Saul. No one dared to face the giant, but with God's help, David stood up to him. He killed Goliath with a stone thrown from his sling. King Saul made David a leader in his army.

When the army came home after the battle, people came out of their houses. They danced and sang in the streets. Everyone was happy. The people loved David. Everyone said how brave he had been. King Saul was very angry. He was afraid the people would make David king in his place.

From that time, whenever King Saul saw David, he became angry.

One day, the King threw a spear at David to pin him to the wall. David ran from the room. David became very unhappy living at the palace. He became afraid of King Saul.

Jonathan, the King's son, was kind. He was a good friend to David. They made a promise to each other that, what-ever happened, they would always be friends.

David wanted to leave the palace. He was afraid King Saul would kill him. But Jonathan did not want him to go. "My father will not hurt you," he said. "He always tells me what he wants to do."

But David was still afraid. He knew that he was in real danger.

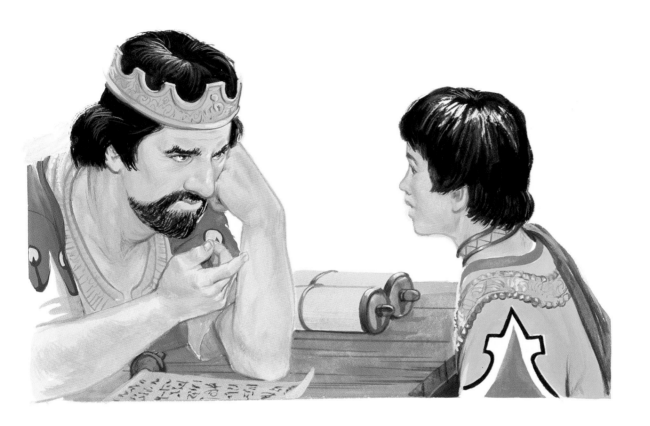

King Saul came to hate David. He told Jonathan to kill him. But Jonathan loved David and so he made a plan.

"In a field not far from here, there is a great stone," said Jonathan. "Go and hide behind it. In three days, I will come with my servant and shoot three arrows by its side. If I say to my servant, 'Go and find the arrows, they are beside the great stone,' then you will know that all is well. But, if I say, 'Find the arrows, they are ahead of you,' then you will know that there is great danger. You must go away."

So David hid behind the great stone. Jonathan went to King Saul. He begged him not to kill David. King Saul did not listen. He became very angry. He threw his sword at Jonathan, but it missed him.

Jonathan ran from the palace, calling his servant. He went to the field near the great stone. Soon his arrows flew through the air.

"Find the arrows,"
called Jonathan.
"They are ahead
of you!"

David heard and he was very sad.
The servant found the arrows.
Jonathan sent him home.

Then David came out of his hiding place. He put his arms round Jonathan.

"My father is so angry. I am sure he plans to kill you. You must go away," said Jonathan. "Hide far away from here. You must remember our promise. We shall always be friends."

David ran away. He found a cave near the desert, where he lived for a long time.

Other men who were afraid of King Saul joined David. He became their leader.

One day, someone
asked to see
David.

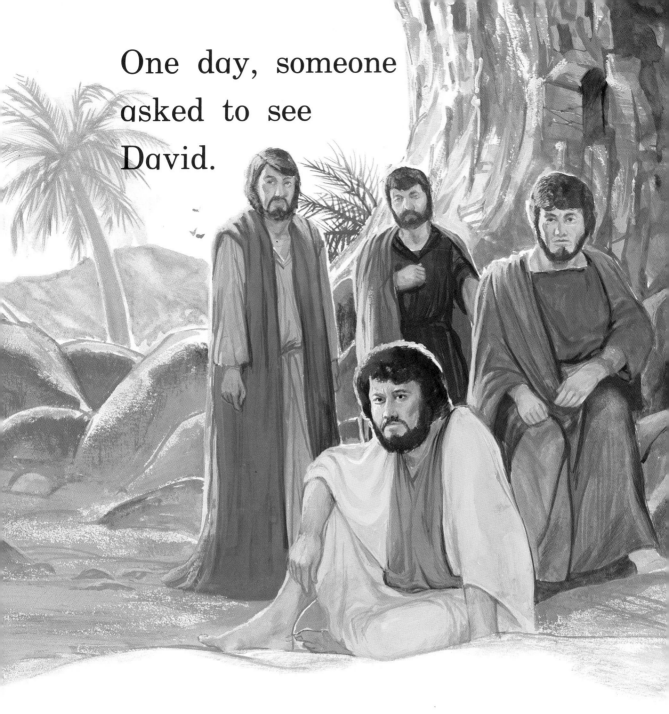

It was Jonathan. A long time had
passed. They were happy to meet
again. They threw their arms round
each other.

"You need not be afraid," said Jonathan. "My father will never find you. One day, you will be king and I shall serve you. Until then, we must part."

Jonathan went back to join his father's army.

Some years later, David heard that there had been a great battle. One day, a soldier from King Saul's camp came to David. His clothes were torn. David could see that he had been in the fighting. He told David that King Saul and Jonathan were dead. He brought the King's crown with him. He gave it to David.

David wept. He was very, very sad. God had made him a king, but David had lost his best and dearest friend.

All these appear in the pages of
the story. Can you find them?

Goliath

Jonathan

David

King Saul